VULTURE

A modern allegory on the art of putting oneself down

by Sidney B. Simon, Ed.D.

ARGUS COMMUNICATIONS
Niles, Illinois

Cover design by Gene Tarpey
Illustrations by Collin Fry

FIRST EDITION

© Copyright Argus Communications 1977

Printed in the United States of America.

ARGUS COMMUNICATIONS
7440 Natchez Avenue
Niles, Illinois 60648

International Standard Book Number 0-913592-89-7
Library of Congress Number 77-73793
    3 4 5 6 7 8 9 0

To Pamela Goodrich,
who has done so much
to free this world of vultures.

Vulture ('vul-cher) noun. **1**: any of various large birds of prey that are related to the hawks, eagles and falcons, but with the head usually naked of feathers and that subsist chiefly or entirely on dead flesh.

Vultures are bad news birds.

All through history, people have thought of them in connection with death and defeat.

Vultures are big, nasty-looking birds with sharp talons and cruel, sword-shaped beaks. They are usually seen circling high in the sky—waiting, watching—or perched on jagged rocks or bare tree limbs, close to something dying.

For vultures, fierce and scary as they look, are not as brave as eagles or other birds their size. They prefer not to get too close to anything that might fight back. They would much rather pick on the weak and helpless—the dying and the dead.

If at all possible, they would rather not attack anything that shows movement, vitality or a determination to live.

It is these qualities that make it hard to like a vulture. Still, even vultures have a place in nature's plan. They help to rid the environment of dead animals and garbage.

But this book is not about real-life vultures. The vultures we're going to talk about are those psychological vultures, the ones that do damage to people.

You might go a long time without ever seeing a real vulture, except perhaps at the zoo, whereas you will probably meet up with flocks of psychological vultures every week—sometimes every day.

They are up there right now, making lazy circles in the sky over your head. They sit waiting in the tree outside your bedroom window. Worse, you can't just run away from them, for these invisible birds can pass freely through walls and closed, locked doors.

Now you are probably wondering: "Why so many vultures? There aren't many dead animals or piles of garbage lying around our neighborhood."

Which makes you worry about what it is, then, that the vultures are looking for.

Or even worse, *who* they are looking for.

"Who?"

Yes.

"Me?"

Yes, you!

This Book Will Show You How to Keep Vultures Off Your Back Forever

What the invisible vultures are after *is* you, all right. Not your body, it's true—but a very real part of you called your self-image. Self-image is the way you see yourself, your own opinion of yourself, your private self-rating system.

You may be perfectly healthy-looking to everyone else—walking, eating, and talking as you always do. But, if you are putting yourself down most, or even part of the time, it means your self-image is wounded. And that is bound to attract the very *unwelcome* attention of the vultures. Soon they will begin to circle closer and closer, sensing the weakness and lack of life which they like to attack.

Take a few minutes to read the story of how these invisible vultures nearly do away with a girl named Patty. She is a real artist at putting herself down. Watch how one time she does it leads to another in a vicious circle of self-put-down so that her self-image keeps running itself further and further into the ground.

Then I'll tell you about some tested ways to keep vultures off your own back for good. Finally, we'll take a look at some of the many ways in which people of all ages put themselves down—and the price they pay for feeding their self-images to the psychological vultures.

8

Patty and the Vultures

To look at her you wouldn't think that Patty
Putdown had much to worry about. She does
very nicely in school—not Ms. Whiz-Kid, but
with grades consistently average or above; a
nice, pleasantly attractive girl, not beautiful,
maybe, but far from plain and miles from ugly;
not skinny, but again, not what anyone would
call fat.

She quarrels, sometimes, with her brother,
Jack, and hates it when he teases her,
especially about boys. But her family is—by and
large—a happy one. In fact, Patty has no big
troubles at all—with school, with her mother
and father, with life in general.

But Patty has one big problem with a capital
"P"—*herself,* Patty.

And Patty is scared. She is threatened every
day by a whole flock of vultures that circle

overhead every waking moment. They sense a weakness in Patty that drives them crazy to get at her, to tear at her opinion of herself. They want to sink their sharp beaks and talons into her self-image; to rip and destroy it completely.

Take today.

Patty wakes up and for a second she doesn't move a muscle or open an eye. But the flock of

vultures who roost on the headboard of her bed know that their breakfast is on the way. They shimmy their wings and shift their feet in their own vulture way.

Patty opens her eyes, looks at the clock and says, "Oh, what a nerd I am! Why did I sleep late again? Now it will be the mad rush bit. Can't I do anything right?"

Just the sort of thing the vultures like to hear.

13

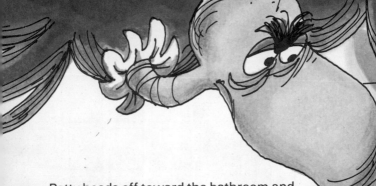

Patty heads off toward the bathroom and slips on the hall rug. She has a few harsh words for the rug, but even nastier things to say to herself.

"Clumsy, stupid klutz! You'll trip on the way up to the stage at graduation—that's providing you ever manage to pass enough courses to graduate."

The boldest of the vultures makes a quick dive and nips off the tiniest part of Patty's self-image.

In the bathroom, Patty takes a sleepy-eyed look at her face in the mirror. Now nobody, not even movie stars, look their best when they've just gotten out of bed, but from Patty's reaction you'd think that it was King Kong's reflection she was staring at.

"Look at that, will you! If you've got a strong stomach. A face that only a plastic surgeon could love—or Frankenstein's weirder younger brother. My nose gets bulbier every day; my lips are too thin; my ears look like catchers' mitts— and my chin is crooked."

In spite of the splashing water and scrubbing toothbrush, three vultures dive like fighter planes and score direct hits on Patty's self-image. But Patty isn't through with herself yet.

She spots the beginnings of two pimples which seem to grow redder while she watches. "I've got to cut down on those brownies and Cokes," she tells herself. "And remember to wash my face with soap before going to bed." Oddly enough, the vultures keep their distance. They thrive on self-put-downs but not on plain old honest facts—things that are true and problems that something constructive can be done about.

But they flutter in anticipation when Patty goes back to her bedroom closet to pick out something to wear to school. They've caught this act before.

"That dress makes me look like a fullback. . . .

"When I wear this old stretched-out orange sweater I look like a sack of potatoes. . . .

"If I wasn't a mental midget, I'd have remembered to pick up my blue sweater from the cleaners. . . . It's the only thing that really goes with these jeans. . . .

"But I really don't know why I worry about it at all—whatever I put on, I'll look like the BEFORE in the magazine ads."

All the while, the vultures are having a ball. With her defenses completely down, they feel safe to show off. They execute loop-the-loops and outside rolls and figure eights right under Patty's nose—taking off chunks of her self-image at will.

16

By the time Patty finally picks out an outfit she finds less gruesome than any other, her mother has gone off to work. Patty goes to the kitchen and reads her goodbye note chalked on the blackboard and sees the lunch she took time to pack for her.

"I'm such a great daughter!" Patty moans. "I can't even bother to get downstairs in time to say a few words to Mom. But she's always got time for me."

Which leaves her so distracted that when her dad comes in to give her a hug before he leaves, all she can manage is a limp little squeeze in return. He doesn't appear to mind, but he isn't out the front door before Patty is on herself again.

"What a way to treat Dad—like he was a piece of furniture to be dusted off. I'm a real winner, I am!"

The vultures dive, but suddenly pull up short, sensing something dangerously constructive about Patty's silent resolution to do better next time in responding to the two people who love her most. Determination shows life, and vultures, you will recall, are afraid to attack where there's any sign of life.

Patty pours herself a glass of milk and is just about to put the carton back inside the refrigerator when Jack, who is running even later than she is, rushes by and pushes the door against her arm. The carton slides from her fingers. Milk splatters everywhere.

"You're even clumsier than I am," Patty yells at Jack. "I can always count on you to make things worse. Don't think I'm going to clean up that mess for you."

19

AWARDS

The vultures regain courage immediately and hurry to put on their flying baseball suits. For Patty has just managed to pull off a double play—she has put herself *and* Jack down at the very same time. Both of their self-images soon look like the batter's box after an extra-inning game.

In the hall, Patty sees her math book and kicks herself for forgetting to do her homework. But she suddenly remembers that she had planned to do it in study hall this morning. So, instead of diving, the vultures put on their helmets and goggles in the hopes of getting a better chance outside.

And they don't have long to wait. At the corner, Patty sees her best friend, Grace—as usual. But Grace is walking and *laughing* with another girl—the transfer student who joined their class last week.

"I can tell already. Grace likes that new girl better than she ever liked me," Patty thinks. "But then, who could blame her."

With more room to work, the vultures dive from a higher altitude and use the extra speed to rip off really bite-sized pieces of her self-image.

"Hi, Patty!" Grace says cheerily. "I'd like you to meet Betty. Betty, this is Patty—my very best friend in the whole world, a super brain, a lot of fun, and—as you can see—a super sharp dresser."

Which is, of course, too much for Patty to handle. She blushes a nice shade of red and replies: "This old orange thing? I forgot my blue sweater at the cleaners so I couldn't wear my new gray jeans and I must look like a real . . . ."

But Betty interrupts her. "I think you look just great. I saw that combination of colors in the window of a big store downtown."

Which naturally makes Patty suddenly feel very good about herself for a very rare second or two. The feeling is so strange, in fact, that two vultures who were about to dive at her have a head-on collision in mid-air because they get completely dizzy when faced with such positive thoughts.

Across the street from school, Grace
suddenly stops the three of them with a sweep
of her arm. "Look, I see Tom over there. Patty,
he really likes you—no kidding! He told me so
last Friday. He's a little shy but he wondered if I
thought you'd be willing to go out with him."

Patty, who might as well put out a "Welcome
Vultures" doormat on top of her head, responds
with a flustered: "Oh, he couldn't possibly like
me! He's so smart and popular and good-
looking . . . . If he talked to me I'd get all
tongue-tied."

While the vultures attack with gusto, Betty
and Grace exchange looks. "Sometimes,"
Grace whispers to Betty, "I think that Patty is
her own worst enemy."

In art class the teacher asks everyone to
create an abstract design. "But I'm not
creative," thinks Patty, going into wild panic.
"In fact, I'm not even original. I'm so square I
can't even draw a circle, much less something
abstract."

24

So the vultures show her how by flying some free-form patterns around her neck.

In science, still upset about art class, Patty can't answer a question on how a voltmeter works, even though she had it down cold last night. She hides behind her lab manual feeling stupid for the rest of the class—even though it turns out that nobody else manages to answer the question to the teacher's satisfaction, either.

In gym, where she usually relaxes and has fun, Patty hits the volleyball into the net on her own team's first serve; she yells to herself all the nasty things that none of the other kids on her team are even thinking about.

Music class—Patty forgets the words to one of the new songs they've been rehearsing and feeds four vultures at once—one for each space on the treble clef.

And in the cafeteria she forgets and buys a brownie and Coke to top off her lunch . . . and then remembers . . . with the last bite and swallow . . . her morning resolution to cut down. A pimple a day, needless to say, doesn't keep the vultures away.

The afternoon actually goes a little better, until Patty makes a wild slip in typing class. Half the keys on her machine suddenly come together in a jam which sticks up over the carriage for all the class to see.

"Stupid idiot!" she groans out loud.

"Never mind, Patty," says Mrs. Waters. "It happens to the best of typists sometimes."

But Patty minds—and she doesn't think she's the best. In fact she's reminded of the time she saw a trained seal try to work a typewriter on TV—and the seal wore a funny hat and tooted a horn at the same time!

Like Mary's pesky little lamb, Patty's vultures follow her home from school. You wouldn't think that after all they'd already stuffed down, they could possibly manage an after-school snack, but that is exactly what they have right after Patty has hers—and then rushes off to the bathroom to weigh herself.

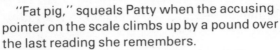

"Fat pig," squeals Patty when the accusing
pointer on the scale climbs up by a pound over
the last reading she remembers.

Patty calms down and checks the mail,
hoping for a letter from a girl she met at

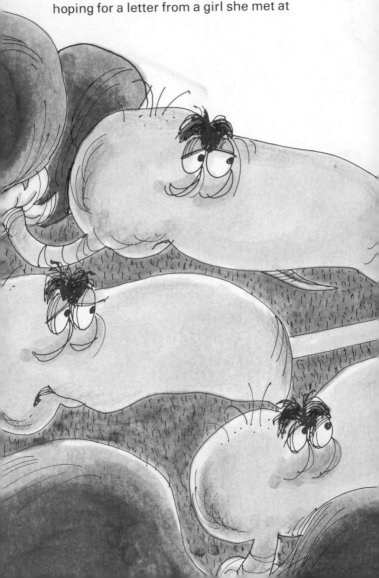

summer camp. But there's nothing but an ad for a magazine which promises to make her look and feel more "glamorous."

Her reaction immediately clears two runways on her self-image for the vultures.

"I *knew* Sue wouldn't write. Out there at camp I was better than nothing—or better than talking to the trees, but once she got home to her *real* friends, she forgot all about me . . . . And it would take more than a magazine ad to make me look glamorous . . . unless they have an instant miracle department."

And so it goes with the rest of Patty's day. At supper she makes up for the Coke and brownie she ate at lunch by skipping dessert, which keeps the vultures at high altitudes above the ceiling light. But, when Patty's mother asks her if she remembered to pick up her blue sweater on the way home from school, they dive for *their* dessert when Patty calls herself a real bird-brain once again.

Back in bed at last, pulling the covers up to her chin, Patty reviews her own day and finds it all too much like all the days she's been having lately.

"I'm on the road to nowhere going ninety," she thinks, giving the vultures one last crack at her. But oddly, they only flap their wings and head for the roost on the headboard of the bed.

Not because they are full—vultures never get enough to eat.

But because there's nothing much left of Patty's self-image.

So, having put herself down about as far as she can go, Patty falls asleep.

Let's hope she likes herself better in her dreams.

Is Patty so unusual? Does she put herself down more than most people? Is there a little bit of Patty in you?

Vultures Go Home!

Nobody can wave a magic wand and get rid of
Patty's vultures for her overnight. They'll be
back on the job bright and early the next
morning—and the next. Poor girl! If there were
some sort of handy product at the
supermarket—a big can of VULTUREOFF—
we'd rush right out and get it for her.

But you can't dispose of these invisible
psychological vultures as easily as that. For one
thing, you can't really get rid of them all at
once. They are smart, too cagey—or rather too
sharp to be caged and carted away in any
instant trap. They have a way of knowing when
you're coming for them—because they hate
determination and signs of life of any sort,
remember—and simply fly off to hide
somewhere until the next time you stumble and
put yourself down. As soon as they sense the
least little hint of negative thinking about
yourself they come swooping back. It's like they
had a wiretap or an electronic bug implanted
in your brain.

What you have to do to get rid of these
vultures is get at them a little at a time, trick
them into flying too close when you're ready for
them. It has to become a habit—which
is something you learn to do without
really thinking about it.

It's called plucking the vultures. And you do it feather by feather. When you've got enough feathers off, the vulture starts to shiver and it finds it harder and harder to fly and almost impossible to dive for your self-image with any sort of control. Finally, the vulture just gives up and goes off to look for a softer touch. Nothing is more helpless or silly looking than a plucked vulture.

Four Easy Steps

So how do you go about the vulture feather-plucking job? Here are some simple but effective ways:

1 You pluck feathers every time you feel good about yourself. If you were to sit down right now and appreciate just a few things about yourself, you would see the whole floor littered with feathers.

Like the way you made yourself go down and try out for the school newspaper reporting job in spite of being scared to —and how much you enjoyed seeing your name in print.

How you managed to stop that stupid argument between your two best friends by reminding them how much you liked them both—and how much they liked each other.

Like the way you managed to get to the library after school to look up that reference for your social studies paper, in spite of all the other homework you had to do.

Now this may seem like bragging, and we've all been taught never to brag about ourselves. But you can't have a good self-concept without knowing that you're a good person. That isn't really bragging or tooting your own horn.

It is, however, very much worth trying— especially since some people never really take time out to appreciate themselves, even once in a lifetime. Turn off that negative, critical little voice of modesty for a few minutes and recite as many good things about *you* as you can think of.

For a change, instead of all the times you let
your parents down, think of the times when you
did do something—and even something extra
and thoughtful. You may have forgotten to take
out the trash twice last week, but you did rake
the leaves without being asked last fall, and you
shoveled the snow faithfully, and you did clean
the bathroom . . . and you did . . . .

Did—that's the big word.

Such positive lists confuse vultures, make
them dizzy so that you can get at their feathers.
Vultures live on self-put-downs, remember,
and when you start thinking *dids* instead of
didn'ts, it is usually more than they can handle.

2 In our age of TV toughness and quick comebacks, it may sound like I'm being phony when I say that

you pluck feathers every time you say something true and good about another person.

Please believe me: it's my professional experience that it is far from phony—it is the real thing.

Vultures are not concerned about handing out gold medals to those who think kind thoughts. They are concerned for their very lives when they hear positive comments: to them, they are as deadly as anti-aircraft missiles.

But be sure that what you say is more than just a breezy compliment. Feathers fall only when what you say is genuine and really adds to other people's opinions of themselves— something they can nail tightly onto that list of good things they are able to recite to themselves in private.

After all, it must be true if someone like you has told them it is so. They didn't just make it up—it came from another person they like, admire, and trust. Positive comments restore and mend self-images. They reverse that cycle of self-put-down we mentioned earlier, and turn it into an upward spiral that gets bigger and better as it rises. Positive comments even add a layer of vulture-proof armor plate which protects when people are alone and feeling negative about themselves.

And, the best part is that when you see how good it makes another person feel to be on the receiving end of an affirming, positive statement, it actually makes you feel better about yourself. A sort of reverse chain reaction. . . . "Feathers keep falling on my head. . . ."

3 You pluck feathers every time you block a self-put-down and start thinking positively. That's where learning to make it a habit comes in. Every time you recognize that you are feeling sorry for yourself, thinking you are down on your luck, worrying about your appearance or abilities—and stop it—you are forming the habit of breaking the depression cycle. Every time you refuse to swallow one of those self-aimed zingers about how big your nose is, or what a forgetful dimwit you are— that's when you begin to pull vulture feathers as fast as the movie theater machine makes popcorn.

I said these steps are easy, and they are. But this one takes some practice. When you're alone and sliding into a self-put-down mood you've got to look out for the warning signals and cut them off at the pass. Call in the cavalry—throw up an imaginary gun and pretend those vultures are so many clay pigeons. You build up your positive habit by turning off that nasty voice that tries to get you to brood about things that are only your *opinion* in the first place.

There's a famous prayer credited to St. Francis of Assisi that might help to make the point here. It goes like this:

God grant me the power to accept what *can't* be changed,

The courage to work at what *can* be changed,

And the wisdom to know the difference between the two.

4 We talked about turning things around—reversing. Well, my fourth rule is that you pluck feathers when you learn to turn your head around and use the force of the old, negative way of thinking about yourself to run over self-put-downs and work at making positive points. This is a sort of mental judo exercise you use on yourself, using the power of the attacking vulture's dive to run him into the ground instead of yourself.

Here are some quick examples of what I mean:

Say: "I used to believe that I wasn't popular enough. . . ." Or, "I used to believe that I didn't do enough around the house to be considered a good son. . . ." Or, "I used to think that I could never remember the dates in history class. . . ."

Go ahead, make up some that apply particularly to you.

It's how you *finish off* such sentences that gets the feathers off the vultures' wings. Even starting a sentence with, "I used to believe . . . " sends them into a tailspin.

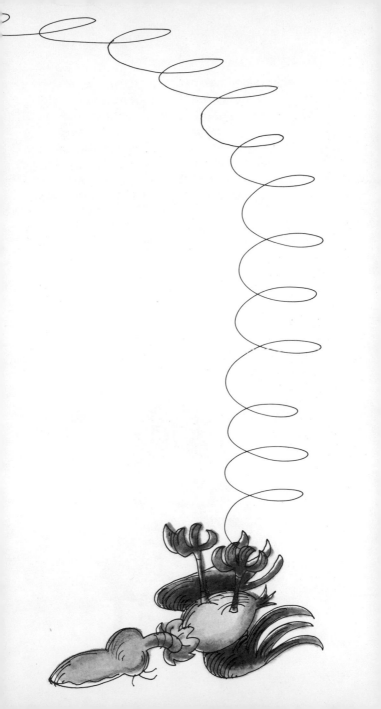

"I used to believe that I wasn't popular enough, *but now I feel sure that people who take the time to really know me actually like me and want to be with me. After all, I do have friends. If I work at getting to know the new girl, I'll have one more.*"

"I used to believe that I didn't do enough around the house to be considered a good son, *but now I feel sure that with just a little more effort I can pull my share of the load and no one will complain. My parents actually seem to value and appreciate me.*"

"I used to believe that I could never remember the dates in history class, *but I know that I can remember lots of things that are important to me. I know every word of all the songs in my favorite record album—and that's quite a headful.*"

Self-put-downs are not limited to young people, by any means. Take the case of this older woman who managed to reverse her feeling of worthless self-pity.

"I used to think that nobody from our church bothered to call and offer me a ride on Sunday because they thought I was just a bothersome, disagreeable old lady who didn't matter—*but now I realize that it wasn't anything personal, but that nobody realized I had no way to get there. Once I mentioned it to a neighbor I haven't been without a ride since—and people actually seem to enjoy picking me up and talking to me.*"

HOLD IT!

Do I hear somebody complaining that those sound like plain old cop-out sentences?

The vultures certainly would like to have you think that they are cop-outs. But they definitely are not. Actually, they are just one more example of how wary you need to be because the vultures are very clever. You have every right to believe in your turnarounds and to use them to build the habit of positive thinking that will lure the unsuspecting vultures close enough to pluck their feathers. The fact is that reversing self-put-downs can make life better for all of us.

Please note that all the turnaround statements have the hard steel of truth in them. There has to be a solid core of truth or they won't work. Look at them closely. Most people can't bring themselves to make that first turnaround in their heads. (The first example.) They spend too much time dwelling on all the people who they think don't like them. They never bother to count up—with the same strong feelings—the people who do like and love them.

We human beings have a strange way of losing our balance. We can sit and listen to ten different people in a row say something good about us, and then hear the next say something negative—and the last is the only one we remember. Instead of saying, "Well, if the score is ten to one, I'm way ahead"—and that's enough to win any hockey game with the vultures—we act like we've lost the game.

Look at the second of the reversals. Here the feather plucking involved a positive plan for doing just a little more work around the house in the future. Positive plans make you feel more comfortable with yourself than just sitting there moaning. You are dealing with something that can be changed.

And the third example is just as useful. It is a way of making sure that you keep track of what is good about you. You *do* have a memory—you've seen it working for you, almost unconsciously. You must, therefore, have a memory and maybe a pretty good one. In fact, as you get to liking yourself a little better—having plucked a few of your personal vultures down to the chilly, bare nub—you may find that it is actually easier to remember those history dates. Why? Because you've freed a big part of your mind for more useful jobs than round-the-clock work at putting yourself down.

Join the Club

There's just one more thing you should know about vultures before you make your own extinct.

Where did they come from in the first place?

Did you know, for example, that there were no vultures around your crib when you were a baby? Babies think they are about the best and only act in the show. They have no doubts whatsoever that they are beautiful, smart, popular, and loveable. So where do the vultures come in?

They come from only one place. They grow out of other people's criticisms, from the

negative responses to what we do and say, and the way we act. People tend to remember these negative things, as was noted, far longer and far out of proportion to the good things they hear about themselves. And so they add them up and gradually begin to believe that there is more bad than good about themselves. Every time we add up enough negative feelings about a particular area of our looks, our brains, or whatever, we have made ourselves a vicious vulture.

And this is a crying shame. It means that we should all learn to be far more thoughtful and gentle with each other. It means we should learn to limit, soften, and generally be very, very stingy about firing off put-downs about others or ourselves. Once we realize how much it hurts to be on the receiving end of a put-down, we will begin to think of them as bullets—bullets that find their mark and stay inside to fester, burn, and infect.

All of us are more easily wounded than we like to admit. It is part of the price we pay for being a real human being. Even the toughest,

thickest-skinned person you know has no defense against the deadly zingers we fire off at each other without thinking.

And the hardest bullets of all to deal with are the ones that come with laughter—the banter and joking around that so often hurts. And we don't even have the comfort of showing our hurt because we have to be a good sport and laugh at our own wounds.

There is a direct relation ("I used to think that I could never understand equations. . . ") between the number of vultures we support and feed and the number of negative criticisms we have counted up and taken to heart. None of us can undo the past that easily, but all of us can be aware of what we say and do in the future.

So how about joining the antivulture club today? Make a resolution to be more aware of how important it is not to put yourself down. Follow that with an equally strong determination not to put other people down, either. We all have faults. That's just part of life. But learn to identify strengths as well, and then build on them. This way faults and weaknesses lose their place in the spotlight and can be overcome by being overcome, one step at a time.

The price of membership in the antivulture club is cheap: **Pluck the feathers off the first vulture that makes a dive at you!**

The Great Self-Put-Down Hunt

We've just seen how the vultures went after Patty's self-image, how they circle and swoop and dive at her in the hope of nipping and shredding it to pieces.

As I said, self-image is the way we see ourselves. Other people may see us in a completely different way. Patty's friends certainly didn't think of her as being unattractive, dumb, and klutzy, but that didn't seem to help Patty very much.

Because, for better or worse, the way we see ourselves is the only one that really counts. It's our self-image that causes us to act and think the way we do in all sorts of situations.

It's bad enough when other people put us down with critical words and cruel comments— there's enough of that going around. But lots of people specialize in putting themselves down before anyone else gets the chance. And the self-put-down hurts just as much. More, really, because while you can get away from the other people who put you down, you can't run from your own personal put-down vultures just by going some place else. As you've just observed in Patty's case, they follow you everywhere.

In the following short "case histories" watch how people put themselves down and let the vultures work at destroying an already shaky self-image.

Bill

Bill, who is ten, is shortstop for his Little
League team. He is a real ace in the field,
seldom missing a ball hit between second and
third or blowing a throw to first. Unfortunately,
the first time Bill came to bat he struck out,
which is hardly a disgrace. But it was to Bill,
who called himself a hopeless clown and a
disgrace to the team. The next time up he hit a
weak grounder and got thrown out and, while
nobody on his team said a word, Bill threw his
bat down and hung his head in self-disgust.
"What good am I to the team if I can field and
never hit?" he asked himself. "I'm hopeless.
They'll be looking for another shortstop by the
end of the game."

And, while the coach didn't begin to think
about replacing Bill then, he eventually did.
Because everytime Bill came to bat in the next
six games he was busy telling himself, "I know
I'll blow it. The pitcher knows a soft touch when
he sees one. It wouldn't matter if he threw
me a basketball, I'd figure a way to miss it
somehow."

Finally, because they kept losing close games
in which even one base hit from Bill would have
provided the winning margin, the coach took
Bill out of the starting lineup.

"Just till we can get you through some
special batting practice, Bill," he told him.

"It won't help, coach," Bill told him. "I'm
hopeless."

Do you think any amount of practice will help Bill?
If not, what will he have to change or do?
What do you think the coach should do to help?
If you were Bill's friend, how could you help him?

Jane

Jane, twenty-six, has just landed a job as an assistant editor at a publishing house. She was selected from more than thirty applicants by the editor-in-chief. She had top grades in college and has a masters degree in English from a very good school. She worked briefly as a reporter and copy editor for her local newspaper before applying for this job. The newspaper gave her an excellent recommendation and sent clippings of some of the stories she had written to the publishing house. But Jane feels very uneasy in her new office at her big desk sitting in her expensive chair. "They couldn't possibly have chosen me because of my ability or record. Not with all those other highly experienced people applying. I don't really know what they expect me to do and I doubt that I'll be able to do a really professional job. . . . They must have chosen me because they needed a woman to make it look like they don't discriminate against females. . . . Probably the government was after them. . . . The man they interviewed just before me said he was from Harvard and had already been responsible for picking out a best-seller. . . . They're just hiring me for window dressing. . . . Probably I'll be asked to do nothing more serious than making the coffee and going out for sandwiches. . . . But maybe that's all I'm good for. . . ."

What are the chances of Jane being successful at her new job?
What would you advise Jane to do—quit at once or wait and see or some other alternative?
What's your guess about Jane's having enough self-confidence to handle her work?
What could her boss and fellow workers do to help Jane find a healthier self-image and what does Jane need to do for herself?

Mrs. Cummings

Mrs. Cummings, 54, lived for thirty years in the same house that she and her husband bought when they were married. Now, with their children grown and gone, they have sold their family home and moved to a smaller townhouse in a different neighborhood. Already, Mrs. Cummings misses her few old friends. She has always found it hard to meet people. For years she has considered herself something of a social misfit, relying on relatives and a few neighbors for companionship. She feels she has nothing interesting to say to strangers, that she is basically a dull, uninteresting person and a poor mixer. Here's what happens when a thoughtful neighbor calls her on the phone:

> "Hello, Mrs. Cummings. This is Marge Henderson two doors down. I'm having a coffee and bridge get-together next Monday afternoon and hope you'll be able to come and meet some of your new neighbors."

> "Oh, my . . . well, thank you but you see I don't play bridge at all . . . and . . . I am so busy moving in and all . . . . I think I'd better not."

> "Well, that's too bad. You wouldn't have to worry about playing bridge. . . . Actually I planned this party as a special chance to help us all get acquainted with you."

"You shouldn't go to any trouble for me. . . . I mean I don't really get along with strangers very well . . . but thank you for thinking of me. . . . Maybe we'll meet some other time."

What percentage of the people you know seem afraid to meet new people?

How do you think Marge Henderson might feel about arranging another party for Mrs. Cummings?

How could Mrs. Cummings reverse her self-image?

Fred

In the middle of his freshman year in high school, Fred, on an impulse, asked a girl in his math class to go to a movie with him. The girl's parents had made a rule that she could not go out on any one-to-one dates until she was a sophomore. But rather than tell this to Fred she simply said, "No thanks, I don't want to go with you." Fred didn't have to, but he concluded that there must be something terribly unattractive about himself. He didn't ask another girl for a date for the rest of his time in school. Now he has a job as a trainee in a large insurance office and, while he's confident about his ability to think clearly and work hard, he's terribly insecure about his appearance and conversational skills. He is attracted to the girl who runs the copying machine—not only is she pretty, but pleasant and outgoing, with a bright smile and a cheery "Hi" whenever he brings work to her.

"I could ask her to go to lunch, or just to have coffee after work," Fred thinks. "But why should she want to go out with a tongue-tied funny-looking klunk like me. Sure she smiles at me, but I'm sure she smiles at everyone—it's part of her job. I know her kind, she's just waiting for me to ask her out so she can say no. . . . Well, I don't need that sort of deal. . . ."

If you were Fred's best friend, what would you advise him to do?

What do you wish the girl Fred asked out in his freshman year had done differently from what she did do?

How might that have helped Fred?

What are some things Fred needs to do?

Mr. Fischer

John Fischer is a skilled, experienced engineer for a large company. He is creative and has always liked to work without much contact with other people in the company. Ever since he tripped over some big words while explaining a science project he was working on in eighth grade and a few of his classmates laughed out loud, he has felt that he can't express his thoughts and ideas clearly. After many months of hard work he has designed a fine new product for the company to manufacture. The manager asks him to present his plans to a national sales meeting in New York at which the company's president and chairman of the board will be present—a great honor and opportunity for John Fischer. But he tells the manager that he can't go to the meeting because his wife doesn't want him to travel and besides he has a great deal of work to do at home.

What is your honest reaction to the reasons John Fischer gave the manager for not going?

If you were the manager, what would you think? If you wanted to convince John Fischer that he should go to the meeting, what would you say?

Comment on the power of long-past put-downs to affect our present lives.

George

George, sixteen, loves basketball and practices dribbling and shooting whenever he can—in fact he is developing into a first-class player with good speed and the height for the game. But when George was very young he lived in a neighborhood filled with boys older and bigger than he was. When they let him join in their games then, just to make up a team, they would ride him about not being able to hang onto the ball: *"Oh come on, George, try to keep up, will you!"* . . . *"Don't give it to George, he'll only lose it!"* . . . *"O.K. George, I guess we're stuck with you till somebody else comes along."*

Now, two of George's friends who are on the junior varsity watch George sink twelve straight free-throws on the outdoor court after school and after playing a quick pickup game with him and a few other boys, urge him to try out for the school team. "We could really use a guy like you, George—Coach says we need some good new players if we're going to develop a strong varsity next year."

But George refuses. "I could never do it—I couldn't keep up with you guys in the big time."

Should George try out for the team?

What would happen if he didn't make it?

One of George's options is not to try out at all. In your opinion, what would be worse than that?

What are the chances that George will gradually outgrow his self-image?

Martha

Sometimes things appear to be put-downs when they may just be coincidences, but because of a bad self-image, a person turns them into a self-put-down needlessly. Take Martha, 28, who's just moved to a city in the Midwest to take a job as librarian. She's invited to a party at the head librarian's home and arrives to find an apartment overflowing with people. After welcoming her, the hostess drifts off leaving Martha to mix and mingle on her own. Martha is not shy, but she is convinced that given half a chance she will say the wrong thing. *"I'm always putting my foot in my mouth. I'm so anxious to make a good impression that I come on too strong. I have a real gift for making myself obnoxious."*

So, when she finally spots a small knot of people in the center of the room, Martha edges in among them and listens to the give and take of the conversation for three minutes. The group has been discussing a movie which Martha saw and liked. Finally, during a lull in the talk she says: "I liked the picture but thought the ending was a terrible letdown." As if on a signal, everyone looks at Martha and then begins to move away to get a drink, pick up some food, or to talk to a different group.

"There, I've done it again," thinks Martha. "What's wrong with me—I'm a social misfit."

If you had been in that group would you have been offended by what Martha said?

Could it be that she came in on the end of a conversation that was about to break up anyway? If so, why do you think Martha reacted that way?

What do you think Martha will do the next time she finds herself in a similar situation?

Faced with the same situation, many people might simply conclude that they had been snubbed by a particularly rude group of people and let it go at that. Why can't Martha?

Pete

Pete is a tackle on the high school varsity—big, tough, strong. And, as everyone in his family has been telling him for years, clumsy as an ox. As a result of years of kidding, Pete is convinced that he is awkward, graceless—and of course, he's never dared to try to learn to dance. "I'd look like a gorilla on ice," he tells himself. "I'd be laughed off the floor." Still, Pete forces himself to go to the pre-Christmas dance in the hope of meeting some of the girls he can never get up enough nerve to talk to in school. But, as usual, he sits with his friends through half of the evening until the band leader announces a "Turn-Around" dance and one of the prettiest girls in school comes over and asks him to dance. Pete is so flustered that he can hardly do more than mumble a few words in reply to her friendly questions and compliments about his football abilities. They move out onto the dance floor. Other couples are whirling and swishing to a fast beat. Pete takes one or two steps, desperately afraid he's going to crush the girl's feet. He feels that everyone in the place is staring and ready to laugh at him. His legs freeze. He mutters an apology and walks away from the girl, wishing the floor would swallow him up.

In what ways do you think Pete's story
is funny?

People—friends and family—were just
kidding Pete about being awkward because
he was so big. What made him take
it seriously?

Do you think it would do any good if Pete
tried to explain what happened to the girl
who asked him to dance? Would you be
someone willing to do that?

69

Let's Do Something!

Well, we've taken a good look at some of the many ways people put themselves down. And we've explored a few ways to pluck those put-down vultures. Now let's get busy and do something about it. Here are a few little exercises just to get you working on the problem.

1 Make a list or inventory of the things you put yourself down about. Then work out your turnaround or reversal for each of these self-put-downs. Go back over your list regularly and see how many of those put-down vultures you've plucked for good!

2 Make a log of the put-downs you dish out to yourself over a day or two. Keep track of each of them. Then again go to work on developing a reversal of them. Make a new log after a week or ten days. See if you can't cut down on the number of put-downs you are giving yourself. But don't get discouraged. We all—even the most confident of us—hand ourselves some nasty put-downs from time to time. The important thing is to keep working on those reversals so you don't let those vultures get the better of you.

3 Go on a put-down hunt. Take a particular time of day—a lunch or coffee break, a school recess, or perhaps even a party— and check out how many times the people you're with hand themselves and others put-downs. Aren't those put-downs destructive? After a couple of hunts like that, you will be much more conscious of the damage put-downs do, and you'll be on your guard against those vultures. In fact, you can turn a put-down hunt into a regular vulture pluck.

Yes, those psychological vultures are everywhere. They leave an enormous trail of human hurt and injury. Each of us needs to be constantly on the watch to keep those diving vultures off our backs. And we can do it by sticking up for ourselves, by reversing our self-put-downs, and by helping other people to see how beautiful they are. The stakes are high. Very few people walk around vulture-free. We cannot afford to let that waste and damage go on. Join us in a great campaign to pluck vultures wherever we can so that all of us can march on through our lives with heads held high.

Learning Magazine

Dr. Sidney B. Simon conducts workshops in values clarification and personal growth in major cities throughout the country. If you would like to receive an announcement and be put on the mailing list, please send a self-addressed, stamped #10 envelope to:

Dr. Sidney B. Simon
Box 846
Leverett, Mass. 01054

We hope you've enjoyed this Argus paperback. Argus has many other titles by prominent authors and we would like to tell you about them. Just detach and mail this card with your name and address.

YES! Send me the *complete* brochure of Argus books.

Name _____

Address _____

City _____ State _____ Zip _____

Psychology   Values Clarification   Self-Help

Personal Growth   Career Guidance   Inspirational

A Complete Guide to your Bookstore's Argus titles.

ARGUS COMMUNICATIONS
7440 Natchez Avenue
Niles, Illinois 60648

Attn: Book Division